TOWARD A NEW CHRISTENDOM

CHRIST THE KING

M. T. R. LAWRENCE

TOWARD A NEW CHRISTENDOM

through
the Arts, Radio, Libraries
and Education in
The Home of the Working Christ

ILLUSTRATIONS BY PAUL A. LAWRENCE

Many Adapted from Famous Paintings

PAL

PAL
PRESS

P.O. Box 487
San Anselmo, CA 94960

NIHIL OBSTAT:
Reverend Milton T. Walsh

IMPRIMATUR:
+ The Most Reverend John R. Quinn
Archbishop of San Francisco, California

ISBN 0–938034–05–7

Printed in the United States of America
First Edition

Lawrence Library Cataloging in Publication Data
Based on Lynn's *An Alternative Classification for Catholic Books*

Lawrence, Madeleine Therese R   , 1915–
   Toward a new Christendom through the arts, radio, libraries and
education in the Home of the Working Christ.
   Includes bibliography.
1. Catholic Action   I. Title

BQT 3518   261   81–84244   ISBN 0–938034–05–7

DEDICATION

To the late William A. Keating, S.J., who loved the Church and the Mother of the Church, Our Blessed Lady. It was he who encouraged the author to prepare for publication the original work under the title which he gave it, "Home of the Working Christ." The "Dream" part was published in *The Y.C.W. Voice* in 1947. Thank you, Father Will.

CONTENTS

FOREWORD

With each passing year the need for a really effective apostolate to this poor post-modern world becomes more evident. The techniques of communication have never been more prolific and sophisticated; yet, what is it that is actually communicated for the most part but yet more satiety and more despair. There is clearly need here for some *work*—work that is at "home" with the truth and the joy of that truth.

With the simplicity and verve of a genuine apostle, Miss Lawrence describes the "home" where this work should go on, where the inter-connecting arts and avenues of communication should be worked over and readied for the waiting world.

It is indeed a *work* that she describes here—work of immense import for the apostolate. But she describes it in the ambiance of "home"—which means that there is love here and the light of truth that always accompanies love.

Both the challenge and the attraction of the true apostolate are heightened by this little book. May its quiet perusal lead the reader to a firmer hold of the one object and source of all apostolic labor: the Home—or Heart—of the Working Christ.

Robert I. Bradley, S.J.

INTRODUCTION

There is a need today for God Our Father, God the Son Our Lord Jesus Christ, and God the Holy Ghost our Sanctifier to be made known to all peoples of the world. He is too little known, too little loved and too little followed.

It is for this reason that we publish an idea which may be a means to this end—evangelization through all modes of action under the title "Home of the Working Christ."

TOHU W'BOHU
(Chaos)

THE SCENE TODAY

A POST-CHRISTIAN SOCIETY

This little work is addressed to the Christian remnant, who although born long after Christendom had disappeared, were born into a Christian society. It is to be hoped that some of the post-Christian society will see the light and join in the move toward a new Christendom.

Our forefathers built a nation founded on Christian principles. But there were, of a later generation, those who wondered, at seeing a moral disintegration, if it would exist long enough to celebrate its bicentennial. It has survived, but continues its moral decline. It is in such a state of moral decay, with abortion on demand sanctioned by the highest court of the land, pornography and sexual abuses rampant, and education without God, in which moral relativism brings about a confusion and skepticism, which if not reversed will be the death of the nation, and find its people ripe for a Communist take-over. As a nation the people have lost all sense of sin.

What of the Church in America? As a child in the Church, I never dreamed that I would enter a period such as that which now exists. A period of "I will not serve." I knew nothing of modernism which went underground at the turn of the century, and which has now come to the surface with new aberrations, and now is known as neo-modernism.

We see abuses in the Liturgy with no effort of those involved to correct them, even when they are spelled out as in the recent document from the Congregation for the Sacraments and Divine Worship entitled "Inaestimabile Donum." The word "authority" is considered passé, and a "do your own thing" attitude has taken its place. Or, it may be that the bottom level becomes the "authority" pressing its decisions on the whole, through a so-called democratic, or consensus approach.

The above are but two points in the over-all picture.

An aside—In the 1930s a man in the Northwest apparently saw the trend. As I recall my father's recounting of a Holy Names Conference in Seattle, the speaker made a statement which the Church holds and its members believe, because Christ promised it. The statement is to the effect that the Church will survive until the end of the world, and that the gates of hell will not prevail against it. But the speaker added something of significance, which I think all would be well advised to consider. Yes, the Church will go on but will we, will we go on in the Church, or words to that effect. The speaker advanced the idea that the Church could be destroyed in the United States, or any other nation, including all of Europe, but this would in no way negate Christ's words. He proposed that in the future we might even have a Chinese pope. Perhaps he even suggested that The Vatican might be in China. However, this speaker was speaking prior to the take-over of China by Communist forces. His main point was that the Church will survive some place. I feel sure he was trying to promote action among his hearers so as to retain and build up Catholicity here.

We may yet see the Asian priest, the African priest offering the Sacrifice of the Mass in our Churches here in the United States in greater numbers, as the decline of priestly vocations continues, or if not reversed.

We need to rebuild the Church in America, on the Rock that is Peter, our now gloriously reigning and beloved Pope John Paul II. Long may he reign.

It is not only with love for country, but for all men, that they may know Christ, live according to his law of love and rejoice in a new Christendom, nations operating under Christian principles for the common good, in and through the Catholic Church, that we write these words. The common good, which includes the spiritual—our final end—is worth working for.

As Our Lady of Fatima requested—prayer and sacrifice is necessary for her triumph, and that a period of peace might descend upon the earth. The contemplative life must not be neglected, this is obvious. But in this presentation, we will deal mainly with the action facet of this subject. We need "all hands on deck."

You, dear reader, I am sure, do not want to be under the tyranny of Satan and his henchmen, who have garnered subjects on the earth. An example, those who care only about what will bring in the most money, it matters little whether it is pornographic or idolatrous.

It was before decadence was as visible as now, that I had a dream, which will be presented in the next chapter. It is a dream which gives one means of bringing peace and true freedom and eternal salvation to many souls.

I hope that you as a reader, will accept the thoughts expressed and do your part to make the dream come true.

SAINT GENESIUS
Patron of Actors

THE DREAM

"This I beheld, or dreamed it in a dream."
—*Edward Rowland Sill*

I must tell you about my dream—But first: Are you a Blackfriar, or a member of the Catholic Theater Movement? Or, do you think it is important for Catholics to get involved in television broadcasting and Catholic movies? Do you believe in adult education? Should study clubs again be a part of the Catholic scene? Secular music groups, and non-Catholic denominations are carrying on the musical heritage which we seem to have abandoned. Should Catholics restore our musical heritage to the Church where religious—and to the concert hall, where appropriate? Could we support a Catholic art gallery, restoring the good, the true, the beautiful? How about a Catholic daily paper? Could it help nullify propaganda and hate in the daily press? Do you use the Catholic lending library in your city, if it boasts of such a thing? Would you avail yourself of its advantages, if such existed?

If you can say "yes" to any or all of these things you will be interested in my dream of—"The Home of the Working Christ."

In my dream, I'm talking to you as we near a modern structure.

"I never heard you say you were interested in acting, but we'll go to the theater first," I said, and added, "from the outside it looks like any other theater, but—"

"These bas-relief figures of men and women on the doors, who are they?" you interrupt.

"Saints", I answer. "Saints of the theater. You've heard the dramatization of the life of St. Genesius, Patron of Actors, haven't you?—No?—You missed that one? Well, he was an actor in the time of the early persecutions in the Church. He was converted and suffered martyrdom. Henri Ghéon wrote a play

17

SAINT CECELIA
Patroness of Musicians

about him entitled 'The Comedian.' We staged it at college. Then there is St. Francis of Assisi, who might be called the father of the theater, although I'll wager he wouldn't recognize the present day theater as one of his children."

"But, this one is St. Cecelia," you object, "she wasn't an actress!"

"No, but she is the patron of music and this theater is dedicated to serve not only the Blackfriars, Catholic Theater Guild, and Genesian Playhouse, but it also serves as a concert hall for orchestra, individual artists and operettas. The Catholic movie—there are a few of them you know—has to have a place too. And, also lecturers—they need a hall where more than just a few can hear them."

"Let's see the inside," that from you. . . . "Oh! It's certainly different" you breathe, a little taken back at the no-aisle diagonal layout of the theater.

"Yes, the designers believed in picking up different ideas, where an improvement, so used the idea of Norman Bel Geddes. This is a more comfortable arrangement for the audience as you can see. There is plenty of leg room between rows, so that one may pass through without disturbing anyone. Come, we'll go back stage, and also to the workshops beyond."

"Why workshops?" you ask.

"One is a costume workshop, the other the scenery workshop. The organizations that use the theater have their own stage and costume designers. When a play goes on the road to other 'Homes of the Working Christ' in the various cities, they, of course, take along their own costumes. The costumes are also available to other groups when the show does not go on the road," I explain.

The scene fades out and then we find ourselves in a large lobby, with two etched glass doors to our left, elevators to our right, and two large doors in the opposite end of the lobby. We turn our steps to the doors at our left.

"More saints on the doors?" you query.

"Yes, the doors in the 'Home of the Working Christ' are etched with the figures of the saints. It is like a litany, a litany of

SAINT PETER CANISIUS
Patron of Libraries

patrons of Catholic action in its many forms. I'll tell you about one of these, and the rest?—I know you're going to be interested in our 'Home' and will discover them for yourself."

"St. Peter Canisius, Patron of Libraries (you know now what's behind those doors) is the figure on the left. Many do not know much about St. Peter Canisius, if they've ever heard his name. I'll admit I didn't know about him until a few years ago. Peter Canisius of the Society of Jesus was the greatest influence in Germany at the time of the so-called Counter Reformation. He was indirectly the founder, or re-organizer of forty universities, no small feat you'll admit. And where do the libraries come in? Well, Peter Canisius knew that the university plan would include a chapel, so the library was the first thing in his university plan."

We enter the library and as the doors close behind us we view a large reading room with book-lined walls and tall windows high above. We read some titles as we walk around the room, *Father Brown Omnibus* by Chesterton, McGuire's *Funeral in Eden*, *The Trap* by Jordan, we look up, "Mystery and Detective" captions this section. We move on. *Flesh Is Not Life* by Barth, *The Golden Rose* by Hinkson, *No More than Human* by Laverty, *No Other Man* by Noyes.

"There's good material for your theater," you offer as a suggestion.

"That's right. That's part of the function of the library. The wealth of material in a Catholic library is practically untouched. We have obtained permission from some of the authors to adapt their works to the theater, for television, and for radio too. So, besides being a source of education and entertainment, it also induces writers to adapt material for the various media, as well as, doing original work. From material in this library, the Genesian Playhouse successfully produced *One of Our Own*, a life of Kateri Tekakwitha, the American Indian, whose beatification was in the 1980 Catholic news."

"*QMP-Stories*," you interrupt. "You know I did enjoy getting those when I was in the South Pacific during World War II."

"Yes, and you'll find all of your beloved Chesterton here,

SAINT JEROME
Patron of Librarians

including Maisie Ward's biography which the public library has so cleverly avoided."

And then you think aloud. "I've often wondered why it is that after a great author becomes a Catholic, the public libraries cease to be interested in his works, and his life. However, if any priest leaves the priesthood and writes a book, they latch onto it right away."

"There is an additional point in favor of a Catholic library, in that it supplements the public library. Of course, there is bound to be some duplication. But,—we will be here all day, if we don't get on our way. We'll have to pass up the Reference Department, children's books, and periodicals, and go directly into the Catholic Bureau of Information in the next room." I say, as I rush you through the next door into the physical hub of the building with its switchboard and connecting lines to all units of the building. "Here are the files containing information to answer such questions as: 'I have just moved into the city, and live at South 12th and Pine, what is my parish church? the name of my pastor? and hours of Sunday Masses?' Or, 'I'm going to Prescott, Maine on my vacation and would like to know the names and addresses of some churches there,' or again, 'I have a friend who is ill and must go to San Francisco, would you give me the names of Catholic hospitals there?' My mother, when in a strange city once, went to a St. Luke's Hospital and found to her surprise that it was *not* a Catholic hospital."

"In this office is located the Catholic calendar of the city, to prevent, where possible, the conflict of two or more important events scheduled for the same day.

"Records are kept here of plays available, art exhibits obtainable, speakers on tour and their subjects, etc.

"The Catholic Book and Gift Shop is the next unit on this floor. A Catholic weekly and many pamphlets start on their way from the press room beyond.

"We'll skip these today, and make a tour of the second floor and then one last stop. But, I'm sure you'll come back for a longer survey on your own, another day."

SAINT FRANCIS DE SALES
Patron of Authors

SAINT DON BOSCO
Patron of Editors

SAINT AUGUSTINE OF HIPPO
Patron of Theologians

SAINT AMBROSE
Patron of Learning

SAINT THOMAS AQUINAS
Patron of Students and Catholic Schools

SAINT GREGORY THE GREAT
Patron of Musicians and Teachers

SAINT JOHN BAPTIST DE LA SALLE
Patron of Teachers

SAINT CATHERINE OF ALEXANDRIA
Patroness of Christian Philosophy

SAINT LUKE, THE EVANGELIST
Patron of Artists

. . . Next we find ourselves leaving the elevator on the second floor—ahead are several classrooms—"That adult education question is answered, for we have classrooms for extension courses and study clubs, for the young boy or girl wishing to obtain evening classes and college credit; for the man or woman who isn't interested in credits but wants to know about liturgy or church history. (Really you know the ignorance on the post-Vatican II Liturgy is quite amazing. Many follow the leader who may be promoting abuses, and has never read the documents, to know what is in them. They follow the so-called 'spirit of Vatican II' which is not the real Vatican II at all.) Then there are courses for the laborer, the farmer, and the business man too, with courses on the co-operative movement, credit unions, the social encyclicals, and guilds."

We enter the door to the right and note that there are no windows in the room; before us is an artificially lighted display of the work of twentieth century artists. We have time for only a cursory survey, before we leave the art gallery, but our practical eye notes the bulletin board which lists future displays of religious art, old and new: in oil, water color, and other media, as well as, photography, etchings, sculpture, fabrics, etc.; exhibits of mission work at home and abroad; of farm practices and aids.

As we enter a door on the same side as the elevators we hear voices but we don't see anyone.

"Spooks?" you ask, laughingly.

"No! Just someone practicing over a mike," I interject. "We're in the audience room, or criticism room, you might call it. Our theater groups are interested in radio work and try out their productions and sound effects here before going on the air, either for live or taped broadcasts. We do have tape equipment too. I suppose soon we'll be going into videotape, or disc audio-visual equipment for the television market, as also for classroom presentations, or for private consumption in the home. The other space on this floor is set aside for meeting rooms of Catholic organizations, and for games and dancing," I add.

SAINT GABRIEL, THE ARCHANGEL
Patron of Radio and Television Workers

SAINT CLARE OF ASSISI
Patroness of Television

THE HOLY FAMILY

Fade out—and we find ourselves in the first floor lobby again with the library to our left and the elevators to the right. This time we go through the two large doors ahead.

"Oh, a lovely chapel, the 'Working Christ' has His throne," you whisper to me as we look through the open door.

"Yes, last, but most important of all is the chapel. The altar, as since Vatican II for most churches, is away from the wall. Above the altar is a large stained glass window of the Holy Family, a symbol of Unity and Love. This and all of the stained glass windows are artificially lighted because of the chapel's position in the center of the building. One is of the Immaculate Conception, Patroness of the United States, the other of St. Francis of Assisi, Patron of Catholic Action.

"All workers in the 'Home of the Working Christ' are members of the 'Guild of the Working Christ.' All positions in the 'Home' (theater included) pay a just annual living wage. Full-time workers for the theater are needed to make it a success. Of course amateurs are given an opportunity to try out for minor parts, and those accepted are paid a salary commensurate with the importance of the role.

"The Chaplain of the 'Guild' offers Mass each morning in the chapel for 'Guild' members. There is a special commemoration in the chapel on patronal feasts," I inform you as we leave.

Where is this "Home of the Working Christ?" At present it exists only in my dreams. It is not always as described above, for now it is in a large city with its teeming masses, again it is in a small town, and another time it is on an open plain, or on a hill, or, in a valley. It is a dream composed of several units of the plan above. We leave to an inspired architect the creation of the design.

Paul G. Lawrence

SAINT FRANCIS OF ASSISI
Patron of Catholic Action

REFLECTIONS ON THE DREAM

The successful fulfillment of the dream of the "Home of the Working Christ" looking toward a *true* Christendom presupposes certain things, without which it would be doomed to failure even though it had the appearance of success.

It presupposes a life of prayer for all, and contemplatives among the Religious Orders.

It presupposes that all of its members, no matter in what field, are loyal to the Holy Father and the authentic magisterium, which includes both the ordinary and the extraordinary magisterium. And, on the reverse side of the coin, that they are not tainted with Bultmannism, neo-modernism and the like.

Evangelization and catechesis are understood to be necessary.

All need to have knowledge of the social encyclicals, and any of the Apostolic Exhortations that involve the individual's field of endeavor.

Now we will consider the dream. In order that this dream might become a reality, funds would of course be needed. Perhaps an endowment, subscriptions, or co-operative groups would establish the groundwork. If a Catholic library, theater, publisher, already exists in a city, would that not be a stepping stone to the fulfillment of such a plan? It is interesting to note that there is always a chapel in which the Blessed Sacrament is reserved in the film and book stores established by the Daughters of Saint Paul.

With a "Home of the Working Christ" in each town and village, a national center could be formed, as a clearing house for plays, lectures, book lists, etc. Units throughout the nation could work, each on one portion of a list of worthwhile books or plays. The completed list could be edited and circulated from the national center. Not only are lists of good books and plays important, but lists of those not worthwhile. The latter as a time-saver for busy play producers and librarians. In one summer, a high school teacher read at least one hundred three-

act plays, and a greater number of one-act plays in search of four
that would be usable for an all-male cast. Also, an organizer of
an amateur radio group could not find a satisfactory all-female
cast play in a search of the city's main public library. This was in
a city of about 185,000 people. This search was made after the
male members of the cast were in uniform (World War II) in
what was to be the last play the group gave over the air. How
many play directors did likewise during the same period? How
many mulled over the same plays?

It would be great to have in a national center a Catholic picture
index. Are there representations of all the Patron Saints of
occupations, for example, those that would be appropriate
for a "Home of the Working Christ?"—St. Vitus, Patron of
Comedians; St. Peter Celestine, Patron of Bookbinders; St.
Bernardine, Patron of Communications Personnel; Saint Eligius
and St. Dunstan, Patrons of Jewelers and Metal Workers;
Blessed Contardo Ferrini, Patron of Universities—to name a
few. Some of the above I never read about until recently. I know
nothing of their lives, much less pictorial representations of
them.

Another concern, in the information area, is that of indexes of
published material. Although there is in existence the *Catholic
Periodical Index*, it is insufficient. Access to it is also limited.
Probably many persons do not even know of its existence.
Publishers of periodical indexes must of necessity be selective.
The task would probably be overwhelming if the indexer at-
tempted to index everything.

The last time I looked at the *Catholic Periodical Index* I noted
that although it indexed the *National Catholic Reporter* it did not
index the *National Catholic Register*. *Our Sunday Visitor* was
indexed but not the *Catholic Twin Circle*. A supplemental index
could very well index these missing periodicals, as well as *The
Wanderer*.

The work of producing a supplemental index of periodicals
could be spread around among local or regional "Homes of
the Working Christ." One "Home" could index the *National
Catholic Register*, another *Homiletic and Pastoral Review*, and still

another *Social Justice Review*. There are probably new publications like *Lay Witness*, which have not yet been picked up by the *Catholic Periodical Index*. The indexing done at the local level could be prepared on 6-up masters for duplicating, and could be duplicated upon request for any of the "Homes of the Working Christ" which would request them.

Not only could periodicals be indexed but books too. The advantage to researchers would be great.

Is this just a dream? could it be more than that?—A place where we could work and play together in love—one in the Mystical Body of Christ?

There is so much behind the dream. So many problems to be solved: of hate and war; of the yellow man, the black, the brown, the red man, and—the white man; and our relations one with another.

This brings to mind the words of Reverend J. R. Keane, Servite Father, in his *Marian Vignettes* given on the Catholic Hour in 1939. "Each town and hamlet will have its own patron saint, its own feasts, its own customs and traditions, yet all will be closely united in that one great community which knows no racial or geographical lines, and over which Christ will reign as King and Mary as Queen."

Which comes first?—The Unity of all?—Our program of education among ourselves?—The building with its study and cooperation?

ACTION FOR FULFILLMENT

Perhaps, I have omitted much, but others could fill in, if we work together: the writer, the publisher, the reader, the actor, the producer, the audience, the physical education director, the artist, the artisan, the educator, the farmer, the laborer, the shopkeeper, the maker of laws, the enforcer of laws, the scientists, the doctors, and last, but certainly not the least, our priests and religious, all under the leadership of Christ, through the Church. We could accomplish this dream with the help of the Eucharistic Christ and the intercession of Our Blessed Lady, Queen of Heaven and Queen of the first earthly "Home of the Working Christ." Dear Reader:—Now you know that "Homes of the Working Christ" are not going to miraculously mushroom throughout the United States. We want *you* to get into the act. We assume that besides saving your own soul, you are interested in working for the salvation of others. And, as an American citizen you would like to see Christianity envelope our nation, to see a true Christendom in operation. Would you not like to be a part of that formation? You need not be a disc jockey, an actor, author, musician, or publisher. Where to begin? That is the next question.

Now there *are* some publishing houses worthy of the name Catholic: The Daughters of St. Paul with their St. Paul Editions, and Prow Books to name two. In the United States we have lost Sheed & Ward, P. J. Kenedy, Bruce Publishing Co., Benziger Brothers, and others as Catholic entities, most having merged with others, or been bought out by other non-Catholic publishers.

Also, we do have some orthodox Catholic Colleges beginning to publish.[1] There is not at the moment, to this writer's knowledge, a directory of Catholic publishers faithful to the Magisterium of the Church. However, such publishing houses exist, such as the two named above.

1 See Appendix I.

43

If a Catholic publishing house is in your city or area, how about sending the publisher a copy of this work, and ask it to get into the act. *You* can get into the act by writing to publishers of good Catholic books, asking for their catalogs, and purchasing their publications, either through your local Catholic book store, or directly from the publisher.

The *Catholic Almanac 1979* does list publishers of Catholic newspapers and periodicals. Send a copy of *Toward a New Christendom* to the publisher/editor, in your city or area, asking them to get into the act.

If you can financially encourage groups such as Mary Productions,[2] do this. Or inquire in what other way you may help in their apostolate.

Another thing you might do is to organize a Catholic book review club[3] among your friends or fellow parishioners. Begin reviewing truly Catholic books, in order to encourage Catholic authors and publishers. If your community has a Catholic library, borrow books for review from them. If the Catholic library does not have the book you wish to review, buy a copy and later donate it to the Catholic library. If you have no Catholic library in your community, this would be an opportunity to provide one. Perhaps, if you have no expertise in the area of library technology, a librarian in a local Catholic school would give you the basic help needed. Or, if *you* cannot do it perhaps another member of your book review club could do so. Another thought is an adult education course in librarianship for parish libraries. There might even be a retired librarian around who would volunteer to help. Have the Catholic library in your home, if the parish has no space for it.

There is another avenue, in which our reader may be involved. This is in the entertainment area. There is a Catholic Actors Guild, established to provide services for the actors. The Guild has its chapel. As we would envision it, it would be a Catholic Theater Guild, and would encompass all who are involved in theater, television, radio, and movies. A guild instead of a

2 See Appendix I.
3 See Appendix II.

union. Catholic personnel in these fields (having the technical knowledge) could form their own Catholic movie production, Catholic theater production. And local people could help establish the physical building to bring these Catholic movies to their own area. Start small, then expand.

This writer, for one, used to attend movies once a month or so. But now—seldom sees one movie a year. The response to this might easily be, "But there is television." This viewer, since the advent of television has had twenty-seven years without television in the home. It was seen occasionally in other persons' homes. Even with T.V. in the home, where once I watched one program a week, it is no longer turned on even once a month. Let's have really good movies, theater and television in order to gain new and regain old viewers.

These are just a few suggestions. With a little thought and ingenuity, you dear reader, can see where you fit into the picture.

Now, it would not be financially possible, and very likely not realistic to see the complete complex of the "Home of the Working Christ," as envisioned in the dream, in every town and agricultural area. But, where any of the services already exist in a city, other units could be added. Example, in the Boston area is the headquarters of the Daughters of St. Paul. They wouldn't be obliged to move their publishing house in order to participate. A bookshop or office could represent them. They could participate shall we say, as an affiliate or associate, of the "Home of the Working Christ." Likewise the Catholic Central Union of America, in St. Louis, which publishes *Social Justice Review* could be an affiliate of such a "Home" in St. Louis. The smallest local "Home" should, in the opinion of the author, have at least a Catholic library and information center.

Earlier we posed the question, "Which comes first?"—The unity of all?—Our program of education among ourselves?—The building with its study and co-operation? That question was posed over forty years ago. And, in my considered opinion, we cannot wait for the unity of all. It seems incumbent on all to pray firstly, and at the same time become truly educated in our Faith. As we do this, begin to work for the "Home of the Working Christ:" in order to educate others, and to permeate their lives with good theater (movies, television, radio). Even this is not enough, we need to work for the common good throughout all the various means of livelihood, and in all things that effect the living of truly Catholic family life, to restore that unit of society which is necessary to bring the world out of chaos, to the true dignity, that is man.

We need to promote orthodox religious education at all levels.

We need to saturate the world with Catholic thought and Catholic life.

Thence, all, in individual pursuits working for a new Christendom in which Christ is King, Mary is Queen in the Mystical Body of Christ. So that all may share "Broken Bread for a New World."

ONE FAMILY FOR CHRIST AND THE CHURCH

This chapter was the last to be composed. It developed from the suggestion to include something of a personal nature.

Any number of other stories could be substituted, but this one is written because I know it full well, for it is about the author's own family.

It was an ordinary family with the usual ups and downs, with occupations of school, work, play, and visiting of friends which are normal. It was not in any planned crusade in which we were involved, nor is it a model in its details. Each family with the talents of its own members can fulfill a chapter in the book of life and the work of the Church. It could be in decorating the altar, or taking care of the altar linens, or handling a benefit dinner.

In the family about which we write, there were a father and mother and four children, to which was added eventually a son-in-law and a daughter-in-law.

First we will tell of the conversion of the little girl who would later be the mother. It is expressed in her own words:

"When I was about nine years old, I found a child's prayer book on the sidewalk in front of our home. I sat on the porch steps and read it with great interest. The beautiful prayers and the pictures of the Mass stirred me a great deal. I showed Mother the prayers to be said before and after meals and she encouraged me to learn them. From then on we said them regularly.

"Two of my cousins were sent to the Ursuline Academy in Arcadia, Missouri. . . . Later on I too enrolled there. I plied the girls with questions about their religion and read *Faith of Our Fathers*.

"Later as a day student I attended the Convent of the Religious of the Sacred Heart near home. I was now attending Mass and Benediction, and praying before the Blessed Sacrament. I told Mother Garesche that I believed in the Catholic Religion and wanted to embrace it. She had me secure my father's permission and arranged for my instruction.

47

"To my great joy I was baptised by Father Glennon, later a Cardinal—and received my first Holy Communion in the convent chapel."

Not recorded in the above but found in her memoirs was the following. She thought it would be wonderful if she could believe that the host was Jesus, but of course she could never believe that. However, she prayed to believe, and one afternoon she found herself on her knees in the convent flower garden facing the chapel and believing.

It was a few years later that her mother and baby brother were baptised. This was followed by the baptism of her two younger brothers. Finally her father was baptised.

The husband-to-be met the convert when she was but fourteen and he fifteen. He decided at this early age that she was the only one for him. He was faithful to her before marriage and throughout over 60 years of married life. His mouth was as clean as his heart. I doubt that anything ever sullied his lips and that the worst thing he ever said was in an exasperating moment, and that was "Oh! rats." This when he had just gone to bed after changing the bed of one of his children, all of whom had the whooping cough, and he heard another wh-o-o-o-p.

As a graduate of a music conservatory, the wife, after her marriage, played the organ at her parish church. Later was both choir director and organist. She sometimes had to sing the bass, or was it tenor part? because the man who was to sing the part was late for Mass.

On one occasion, the parish priest said he wished someone would compose a short *Ave Maria* without all the repetitions in the compositions usually sung. It was usually during the Offertory that the *Ave Maria* was sung. Because of the many repetitions the priest would have to stand and wait until the singer finished before continuing Mass.

While asleep one night, a melody came to her, and she awoke, got up and wrote down the melody. She arranged to have it published. The only repetition in her *Ave Maria* was that of "Amen," which was repeated one time.

As the babies came along there was an interruption in her

playing the organ for High Mass. The family moved, after the first child was born. It was after the fourth child was born, if not before, that she began playing for Benediction on Sunday afternoons. Whether the family were on a Sunday outing, picnic, or at one of the lakes in the vicinity, or, just out visiting, there was the rush in to church, where the mother and the children trudged up the stairs to the choir loft. In those days someone had to pump the air for the pipe organ. It was either Dad or one of the children who did this, until the day when a motor was installed to do this work. The children all sang the Benediction hymns with their mother. In later years, when older members of the family were away from home the youngest daughter played for Sunday Benediction.

The mother also taught piano, voice, and, violin for beginners, in Catholic schools.

The father was away on business most of the week, so was not involved much in other church affairs, but on at least one occasion helped build booths for the annual church fair. It was later after retirement that he joined with men of the parish to form a Catholic parish credit union. He was on the board for a number of years and was awarded a commendatory plaque for his service. He was a member of the Knights of Columbus over sixty years. He was also instrumental in forming a group to study Communism under the tutelage of the Cardinal Mindszenty Foundation.

There was much sickness in the family and the eldest son was stricken with tuberculosis. Although this was arrested he was never well again. So we have no further Catholic Action to report from him. But there is one very important statement that he made, and has probably fulfilled in the intervening years. On one occasion he said "People are not willing to carry their crosses, but I mean to carry mine."

The eldest sister had a talent for sculpture. First it was soap sculpture, then, clay sculpture, then in ceramics. Most of the subjects of her work have been of a religious nature. Her work was not a commercial venture, rather being limited to her own home and to gifts. Eventually the rearing of her family left no time for these artistic pursuits. However, what time she had available brought her into work with the Holy Family Retreat Movement. Later when time permitted, she also played the organ for Mass and for Benediction.

She and her husband, since the family are grown, sing in the choir of a neighboring parish. Her husband has for years been a member of the Knights of Columbus, and of Serra International. For over ten years the couple have been working with a group that has a Catholic radio program on the air every weekday following a rosary program.

The younger son, who also has a talent for art, and since childhood has been interested in movies, was during World War II, the official photographer for his battalion. After his return from the Pacific, having read about Fatima while on Saipan, determined to make a film on the Fatima story. His determination was built on the fact that he (mistakenly) thought that Hollywood would not film such a story.

The film was completed with the cooperation of family, neighbors, and friends. This film at one time released under the title of "Peace Plan from Heaven," was of course an amateur film. All who participated in its production were volunteers, unpaid, including the producer. However this little amateur film came pretty close to covering the globe. For during its life copies were purchased by citizens of the countries, or donated for the following countries: United States (of course), Mexico, Wales, India, Philippine Islands, Japan, Germany, Africa, a city in the Caribbean and at least one South American country. It was purchased by a Catholic rental film company in New York, another in St. Louis, and by the Holy Names Society in Seattle, Washington. It was shown on television in Texas. The producer/director/cameraman himself showed it in many schools and parish halls in California, New Mexico and the State of Washington. Subsequently he produced five other films.

Our cameraman/producer, also taught CCD for about five years in the local parochial school.

The author of this book is the youngest member of this

family. She assisted in the library of the high school from which she had graduated earlier. Later she began a Catholic library in her home. When she moved to California she found a parish library already in existence. With other volunteers, she helped staff this parish library for several years.

She and her mother played the organ for the Friday night Holy Hour. The youngest member also played the organ for congregational singing for one or more Masses in the parish church in the city where she was employed prior to retirement.

The husband of the elder daughter, served on the altar as a boy, and into adulthood. He was Master of Ceremonies during Holy Week services, painted the backdrop for the Nativity scene in the church. Since Vatican II has been Lector and was installed as an Eucharistic Minister.

The above activities were the spare-time activities of this family. One can channel spare-time activities into work for Christ and the Church.

Recently, a priest when speaking to a small group of people, asked "How much time do you spend with television?" And added the comment. "One should spend at least the same time for God." His intention of course was time spent at Mass, in prayer, in meditation. But surely this could also include Catholic Action.

Though one's talent may not be artistic or musical there is a place in Catholic Action for whatever talents one may have. May you make the Church the beneficiary of your talents.

A NEW CHRISTENDOM

Will this *new* Christendom be a "heaven on earth?" The answer is "No!" for it would take the angels and saints with God to make a heaven on earth. Man (using the generic term) has a fallen nature, so we'll have no heaven on earth. As one theology professor in a course in the Sacrament of Matrimony put it— "Remember when you marry, you marry *fallen* human nature. And, not only do you marry *fallen* human nature, but you take *fallen* human nature with you into marriage." So, all who live in a *new* Christendom will not only be a part of *fallen* human nature but living in a community of those with *fallen* human nature. However, recognizing this fact, all will do all in their power to work in harmony with their neighbors, fellow workmen, and others with whom they have any social relationships.

Will this *new* Christendom be a utopia? Again, the answer is "No!" Utopias have been attempted in many places at different times, but have failed, have been abandoned.

What then will this *new* Christendom be? It is envisioned as a time when Church and State would cooperate. There would no longer be a separation of Church and State. Both should cooperate for the common good. Bear with me, don't run away. It is not intended that the Church run the State, nor that the State run the Church. Rather that they work hand-in-hand. If the citizenry are of one mind in faith, and in practice of that faith, then the political horizon would also be one.

Errors of the past would be avoided in order that there be an harmonious whole. The State would *not* appoint bishops, or other offices in the Church, nor determine in what geographical area any church official should reside or have area of influence. It would be hands-off. The State would handle affairs of State. The Church would not make decisions in State affairs, but would control the Church's proper functions.

In respect to the State, it cannot remain totally neutral

regarding religion. History can illustrate that where a government may begin in a neutral position it will either foster religion or become anti-religious. We can cite our own nation as an example. Its Founding Fathers built into the Constitution that there be no established State church, thereby taking on a neutral position. This left the individual citizen the option of belonging to the religion of his choice. But today two hundred years later, we find a secularized society that has engendered a stance of total disregard for the religious life of the people. Secular humanism has not by edict, but in actual practice, become the official religion of the land. The Supreme Court has so decided. The refusal to give financial aid to religious schools, based on the so-called separation of Church and State clause has in effect shown an anti-religious stance.

To recapitulate, in the new Christendom period, the State would cooperate with the Church for the common good of its citizens. This as stated earlier includes the spiritual—the final end of man. This cooperation would include the enactment of just laws. Nothing in the law would prevent the citizen from freedom in following his religious beliefs, and, the open profession of his faith in public worship. Nothing in the law would prevent him from the education, either in school, church, or the privacy of his home, that of himself, or of his children. At the present time, although some constitutional governments guarantee these rights and freedoms, in practice many do not allow this freedom. This injustice would be obliterated in a Christian society.

The State would look to the Church for moral decisions, where a moral judgement is needed. If a true Christian society now existed in the United States, the Supreme Court decision of January 22, 1973 would never have occurred. If any doubt as to the morality of a decision could occur, this would certainly be the place and time for a Church decision. One may not do evil that a good might result. The "good" of Roe vs Wade was apparently related to the "privacy of the individual." But the "good" for the individual in this case was infinitesimal in relation to the horrendous evil of killing the innocent which has resulted from the Supreme Court decision. Even one death of the unborn would have been a greater evil than any so-called good accruing to the individual woman concerned. This is one example of the anti-religious stance of a supposed neutral State.

As stated before, the State would not oppose the free exercise of one's religion, neither would it by coercion force anyone to become a member of any particular religion. It was a fact, that in the past, when pagan emperors and kings were converted to Christianity, that all their subjects had to follow suit. Here too, mistakes of the past would be avoided.

Following the Liturgical Year would be part of the daily living of the citizens. Church feasts would be celebrated in the home and will be discussed later when we write of the "domestic church." Church holydays would be civil holidays. This would preclude any discussion, as recently seen, of dropping holydays, or transferring them to Sundays because "many" cannot comply with the Church's disciplinary laws regarding them, i.e., attending Mass and avoiding servile work.

We think of ourselves today as being so progressive. Look back at the thirteenth century, when in some, if not all European countries, there were twenty-four holidays, on the eve of which workmen worked only to 4:00 p.m., and on Saturdays (eve of Sundays) the work day ended at 2:00 or 3:00 p.m. At that time the average work day was from seven to nine hours. Now, in the twentieth century, only those who work a 5-day week have more time off than those of the thirteenth century.

With respect to holydays also being holidays, at the present time, the only persons who can follow this procedure, other than retired persons, are those whose day is scheduled by appointment, such as: doctors, dentists, lawyers, beauty-parlor operators and the like. I know of one dentist, who has never made appointments on holydays of obligation. This has been his practice in almost 40 years in this profession. This leaves him free to attend Mass and abstain from servile work. He apparently doesn't advertise this fact, but his relatives know that these days are always cancelled out in advance.

In the new Christendom, all businesses would be closed on

Sunday even if also closed on Saturdays or another day in the week. The exception to this and the holyday closing would be areas of public safety: fire and police; and transportation services: buses, ships, trains and airlines; and, medical facilities such as hospitals, and nursing homes; and, such businesses as hotels, and utilities. In communities where more than one gas station, restaurant, pharmacy and such like exist in a city or town, they would alternate opening on these days for the convenience of travelers, or in emergencies. Personnel would need to be on hand in National and State Parks, and other resort areas. Arrangements would be made for employees, so they could, at least, attend Mass on Sundays and holydays of obligation.

For the common good, instead of labor unions in opposition to management, there would be functional groups/vocational orders, which could take the names and perhaps the forms of the old guilds. These organizations would be formed within the profession or area of employment, with management and labor in the one guild working for the benefit of all in the group. This program has been established in at least one community in the United States. Other communities, industries, are interested in its methods and successes with the thought of establishing the same system in their area. The laborer could be given stock in the business, or enterprise, as part of his wages, thus reap his percentage of the profits.

Besides the cooperation of the guilds in their own field, there would be social concern of all in the general community life. The fostering of the good and the useful in, not only the theatrical, educational, art and music areas as envisioned in the dream, but in the leisure world. This would include the athletic and outdoor atmosphere of hunting, fishing, picnics, parks, the beach, mountains and other places of congregation, where the citizenry would have concern for all of God's children.

And further, every city and hamlet would have its patron saint. The Christian people would also believe in and honor the Guardian Angel of each city, village, church, state, and nation, as well as, the person's individual Guardian Angel. Further each nation would have Our Lady as a special patron. Many nations already have her under one of various titles as their patroness. We here enumerate those about which we know: Poland—Our Lady of Czestochowa, The United States, Brazil, Corsica and Portugal—Immaculate Conception, Argentina and Uruguay —Our Lady of Lujan, Australia and New Zealand—Our Lady Help of Christians, Brazil—Nossa Senhora de Aparecida, Chile —Our Lady of Mt. Carmel, Dominican Republic—Our Lady of High Grace, France, India, Malta, Paraguay and Republic of South Africa—Our Lady of the Assumption, Hungary— "Great Lady of Hungary", Lesotho (South Africa)—Immaculate Heart of Mary, Philippines—Sacred heart of Mary, Slovakia —Our Lady of Sorrows, the Americas and Mexico—Our Lady of Guadalupe.

We leave the national level.

There would be a new look at the family, the basic unit of society. This new look should be modeled on the Holy Family: Joseph—head, Mary—heart, Jesus though God humbling Himself to obedience to an earthly father and mother. The man of the family would have a family living wage, so the wife could make the home a real home, not just a place to eat and sleep. Children could be given work to do in the home commensurate with their age and ability. For this they would receive *no* monetary allowance. It would be their labor of love for parents, brothers and sisters, a contribution to the welfare of the whole family.

Every Christian becomes by Baptism a participator in the priesthood of Jesus Christ. All the baptised belong to the royal priesthood and cooperate with the ministerial priesthood of the Sacramental ministry. The laity are strengthened in this priesthood through Confirmation and are vitalized in it through the Eucharist.

It is in this "domestic church" that the mother in the home, with the children, under the guidance of the father nourish body and soul. This is done through education and example, and by preparing the children to receive the Sacraments, particularly with reference to participation in the Eucharist. Thus bringing the family unit closer to Christ and closer together, preparing it for the final goal heaven.

As co-creator, with God, the mother and father can produce the greatest masterpiece: the human child.

This Catholic family working and praying together, at least once daily, in a spirit of love and unity is the ideal. This ideal made real, could and would be the means of sustaining Christendom. In addition to praying and working together, the family should have some leisure time together. At least one evening a week should be spent together, perhaps in the home, perhaps visiting friends, relatives, or neighbors, or all going out to the library together, or to a show, other entertainment, or a sports event. A home, with love and cooperation in all things would be a place in which each member of the family would delight.

It's a labor of love to make things. Children can learn to embroider and to knit. It was, I think, the Curé of Ars, who when a child of 8 or 9 years of age was knitting his own socks. With work of this kind one can learn to know the labor and time involved in such pursuits, and thus learn to appreciate such things, and be more concerned about caring properly for them. Men and boys need not be embarrassed to knit, weave, crochet, or do needle-point. In the past, in sanatoriums for tubercular patients some doctors would teach the patients, both male and female, how to knit and how to crochet. A young navy man, injured in Vietnam, learned to tool leather while in a hospital in Japan. This skill was taught to him when it was found he was not as adept at crocheting as some of his navy comrades. Some time past, I read of a doctor in one of our central states, who wove and tailored clothes, not only for himself, but for his wife and children.

The priesthood of Christ, embodied service and sacrifice, and is the model for service and sacrifice in the home.

All of these, around the home activities, would foster a slower pace which is much needed in today's society. During a period in which everyone is occupied with one's own handwork, another member of the family could read to the others. If musically inclined, all with any kind of voice could stand around the piano and sing, or perhaps, a little at home concert could be given by those studying music. Members of the family should not leave all the performing to professionals on television or radio.

How nice, if Mom can bake bread, as well as, cook the meal, and also make clothes for herself and the children.

The following is another thought for the home, embodying the idea of not wanting everything at once, not keeping up with the Joneses. There was an instructor in interior decorating, in an adult education program, who had been employed in Hollywood. He worked for some of the movie stars, the latter could go out and furnish a whole house at one time—But, he said to buy this way one had no appreciation for anything in the house—much better to buy one piece at a time, and select with care. One would have more appreciation. He mentioned a young couple who, when they married, bought all used furniture for their home, or apartment. One at a time the various old pieces would be replaced. These would be purchased on special occasions such as birthdays, Christmas, anniversaries. That year there was one piece of furniture in the front room that "stuck out like a sore thumb" but come Christmas, a new chair would take its place. Doing things this way, fits a Christian pattern of the lesser importance of things of this world, while we can concentrate on the future life.

We would like to leave the purely material at this point to some material representations of the spiritual. It is to recommend that in each home in America there be a representation of Our Lady of America, either by a statue or by a picture. In addition to this, a display of "The Coat of Arms of the Christian Family" might well have a place of honor.[1]

This representation of Our Lady of America, has a story behind it. Whereas, most know of Our Lady's appearance to Juan Diego on Tepeyac Hill near Mexico City and her representation known as Our Lady of Guadalupe of 1531, few probably know of recent apparitions in Ohio.

[1] See Appendix I.

We wish to quote from a booklet *Our Lady of America*, a special portion related to youth.

"Our Lady made known to me that she is particularly interested in the *youth* of our nation. It is they who are to be the leaders of this movement of renewal on the face of the earth. Their ranks will be swelled by the youths of other nations whom Our Lady also calls to help in the accomplishment of this great renewal.

"But the youth must be prepared, and this must be done by instilling into them, not only the knowledge of the Divine Indwelling, but a serious study of It, a living It in such a way that the Divine Presence becomes, as it were, an intimate and necessary part of their life and daily living. From this will flow a great love, a conflagration that will envelop the world in the flames of Divine Charity. This is what Our Lady is working for, because this is the great desire of her Divine Son, and it is to the *youth* of America that she is holding out this challenge. A medal which Our Lady asked to be made is to be their shield against all evil, the picture or statue of Our Lady, the protection of the home, the statue at the Shrine in Washington, D.C., a special safeguard for our country. America, the United States in particular, is being given the tremendous, yet privileged, opportunity to lead all nations in a spiritual renewal never before so necessary, so important, so vital."

As the coat of arms was on the shield of the chief, in early European history, so now can "The Coat of Arms of the Christian Family" be the Coat of Arms for all Christians here in America.

Patronal feasts of each member of the family would be celebrated as festively as birthdays, or perhaps more festively. The liturgical year would also be a part of family life in the home as well as in Church.

Family customs would be encouraged. It is a shame that many national customs from Europe have been lost when people emmigrated to America. Although America is in a sense a melting pot, this should not discourage new citizens from retaining in their homes, customs from the place of their nativity. It would be good to research and revive the native dances, native recipes, whether from Europe, Africa, Asia or an Island country. All customs, so long as there is nothing inimical to the faith should be welcome. The dancing, music, and art of various nations so fostered could be performed or shown as education and entertainment. Such cultural performances can show the good, and diversity of the peoples of the world, while the people have a unity of faith.

It is a foregone conclusion, that in this new Christendom, the "dream" itself would be in full operation.

A new Christendom would bring about a new community spirit, a new neighborliness, a new charity.

The populace would be more imbued with celebrating the Liturgical Year.

Like the Covenant of Old, God will be with His people if they follow His commandments.

Love, true love—the wish, the desire, the prayer, the active participation in, the good for oneself, and for all with whom one comes in contact would be the norm. Helping one another get to heaven would be the *new* Christendom.

A new Christendom would place a new heart in the world, one of flesh to replace that of stone.

TOWARD A NEW CHRISTENDOM

APPENDIX I - - - DIRECTORY UP-DATE - - - 1988

Additions, changes of address and other
corrections and changes

Page 63 - - Stella Maris Books (add publisher)

- - A.C.Prosser,Jr. (change to A. & A.
Prosser)

Page 64 - - Drama of Truth, change to:
Catholic Media Apostolate
P.O.Box 255
Harrison, N.Y. 10528

- - Keep the Faith, Inc. (new address)
810 Belmont Ave.,
P.O.Box 8261
North Haledon, N.J. 07508

- - Ministro-O-Media, Inc. (new address)
P.O.Box 155
Pomfret, Maryland 20675-0155

Page 65 - - Mary Productions (new address)
Alice Tomass Place #212,
Oakdale Drive
Middletown, N.J. 07748

St. Gabriel Media, Inc. (new address)
P.O.Box 255
Farmington, Mich. 48024

Page 66 - - For Our Lady of America booklet
delete Holy Family Center. The
booklet is now available from:

Contemplative Nuns
P.O.Box 445,
Fostoria, Ohio 44830

Under Pontifical Institutes delete:

Rev. Arthur E. Rodgers item.

(over)

Page 66 - - Change the Rev. Msgr. Eugene Kevane
item to read:

Notre Dame Apostolic Institute
Rev. Franklyn M. McAfee, Director
200 North Glebe Road
Arlington, VA 22203 Phone (703)
841-2569

ADDITIONS

BOOKS   Catholic Sales--Books and Gifts
                  12525 W. Lisbon Road
                  Brookfield, Wisconsin 53005

BOOKS   Trinity Communications
AUDIO   9380 Cl Forestwood Lane
VIDEO   P.O.Box 3610
                  Manassas, VA 22110 Phone 703-369-2429
                                      or "   "   2789

BOOKS   Thomas & Karen Loome, Booksellers
                  Old Swedish Covenant Church
                  320 North Fourth Street
                  Stillwater, Minn. 55082
                  (not specifically Catholic, but a
                  source for some out-of-print
                  Catholic books.)

AUDIO &   Eternal Word Television Network, Inc.
VIDEO   5817 Old Leeds Road
TAPES   Irondale, Alabama 35210

AUDIO   Stella Maris Books (see p63 for address)
TAPES

VIDEO TAPES   PAL Press
                  P.O.Box 487
                  San Anselmo, Calif. 94960

MUSIC TAPES   Stella Maris Books (see p. 63
& RECORDS   for address)

Adult   Catholic Home Study Institute
        9 Loudoun Street, S.E.
        Leesburg, VA 22075   Phone: 703-777-8388

K - 12 Our Lady of the Rosary School
Home   P.O.Box J   Phone Janice Smyth -
Study   Haymarket, VA 22069   703-754-2919 or
                                703-754-0819

K - 12 Seton Home Study School
        One Kidd Road   Phone. 703-639-9990
        Front Royal, VA 22630

PONTIFICAL STATUS FOR CATECHETICAL TEACHING

        Magdalene College   See p. 65 for address
        (by Sept 1990, expect to be in a new
        location.)

        Pontifical Catechetical Institute
        50 St. Paul's Ave.,
        Jamaica Plain, Mass 02130
        (Daughters of St. Paul)

SPECIAL ORGANIZATIONS

Page 66. Catholics United for the Faith (new address)
        45 Union Ave.,
        New Rochelle, N.Y. 10801

        Apostolate for Family Consecration
        Box 220   (Special program uti-
        Kenosha, WI 53141   lizing books & video)

        Catholic Truth Society of America
        P.O.Box 6182
        Ben Franklin Station
        Washington, D.C. 20044

        Catholic Center
        721 Second Street, N.E.
        Washington, D. C. 20002

        Latin Liturgy Association
        Dr. Robert J. Edgeworth, Sec.
        P.O.Box 80426, Baton Rouge, LA 70898

Traditional Mass Society
P.O.Box 447
San Juan Capistrano, Calif. 92693

Human Life International
P.O.Box 6013
Gaithersburg, MD 20877-9951

Pro Ecclesia Foundation
663 Fifth Avenue
New York, N.Y. 10022

Morality in Media
475 Riverside Drive
New York, N.Y. 10015

The Maryheart Crusaders   (special work with
22 Button Street   fallen-aways)
Meriden, Conn. 06450

Women for Faith & Family
P.O.Box 8326
St. Louis, Mo 63132.

Catholics Committed to Support the Pope
1718 Connecticut Ave., N.W.   Suite 410
Washington, D. C. 20009

DELETE

p. 63   Christian Classics

p. 65   Cardinal Newman College

APPENDIX I

SELECTIVE DIRECTORY

CATHOLIC BOOK PUBLISHERS AND DISTRIBUTORS

Christendom College
publisher
Rt. 3, Box 87
Front Royal, VA   22630

Prow Books
publisher
1600 West Park Ave.,
Libertyville, IL   60048

St. Paul Editions
publisher
50 St. Paul's Avenue
Jamaica Plan, MA   02130

Catholic Treasures Books
distributor, old and new books
626 Montana Street
Monrovia, CA   91016

Christian Classics
distributor
205 Willis Street
Westminster, MD   21157

Lumen Christi Press
publisher and distributor
P.O. Box 13176
Houston, TX   77019

Stella Maris
distributor, new and out-of-print books
P.O. Box 11483
Fort Worth, TX   76110

Ignatius Press
Distribution Center
15 Oakland Avenue
Harrison, NY   10528

Catholic Library Sources
out-of-print books
P.O. Box A3583
Chicago, IL   60690

A. C. Prosser, Jr.
out-of-print books
3118 North Keating Ave.
Chicago, IL   60641

Our Blessed Lady Victory Mission
distributor
5400 West Vliet Street
Milwaukee, WI   53208

TAN Books and Publishers, Inc.
publisher and distributor
P.O. Box 424
Rockford, IL   61105

TAPES

Cardinal Communications
cassettes
Box 34
New London, CT   06320

Keep the Faith, Inc.
P.O. Box 254
Montvale, NJ   07645

Catholic Books on Tape
cassettes–purchase and rental
P.O. Box 18990
San Francisco, CA   94118

Ministr-O-Media, Inc.
cassettes
c/o St. Joseph's Church
Pomfret, MD   20675

TAN Books and Publishers, Inc.
cassettes
P.O. Box 424
Rockford, IL   61105

P.O.P.E. Publications
cassettes: catechetical and other
P.O. Box 6161
San Rafael, CA   94903

Daughters of St. Paul
video tapes
50 St. Paul's Ave.,
Jamaica Plain, MA   02130

RADIO

Catholic Views Broadcasts
86 Riverside Drive
New York, NY   10024

Christopher Radio Program
12 East 48th St.
New York, NY   10017

P.O.P.E.'s Catholic School of the
  Air
outlet KFAX, San Francisco
P.O. Box 6161
San Rafael, CA   94903

TELEVISION

Christopher TV Series
12 East 48th St.
New York, NY   10017

Father Peyton's Family Theater
  Productions
7201 Sunset Blvd.
Hollywood, CA   90046

Eternal Word Television
  Network, Inc.
Our Lady of the Angels Monastery
5817 Old Leeds Road
Birmingham, AL 35210

Drama of Truth
Box 255
Harrison, NY 10527

St. Gabriel Media, Inc.
P.O. Box 39015
Redford, MI 48239

FILMSTRIPS

Don Bosco Films
148 Main Street, Box T
New Rochelle, NY 10802

MOVIE RENTALS

Daughters of St. Paul
50 St. Paul's Ave.
Jamaica Plain, MA 02130

THEATER SCRIPTS

Mary Productions Guild
royalty free
58 Lenison Ave.
Belford, NJ 07718

CATHOLIC COLLEGES

Cardinal Newman College
7701 Florissant Rd.
Normandy, MO 63121

Christendom College
Rt. 3, Box 87
Front Royal, VA 22630

Magdalen College
R.F.D. 5
Bedford, NH 03102

St. Ignatius Institute
University of San Francisco
San Francisco, CA 94117

Niagara University
Niagara Falls, NY 14109

Thomas Aquinas College
10000 No. Ojai Road
Santa Paula, CA 93060

PONTIFICAL INSTITUTES OF CATHOLIC TEACHING

Rev. Robert I. Bradley, S.J.,
  Director
Our Lady of Peace Institute in
  Catholic Teaching
3600 S.W. 170th Avenue
Beaverton, OR 97005

Rev. Msgr. George A. Kelly,
  Director
Institute for Advanced Studies in
  Catholic Doctrine
St. John's University
Grand Central and Utopia
Parkways
Jamaica, NY 11439

Rev. Msgr. Eugene Kevane,
  Director
Notre Dame Institute for
  Advanced Studies in Religious
  Education
Middleburg, VA 22117

Rev. Robert J. Levis, Ph.D.,
  Director
Center for Catechetical Studies,
  Gannon University
Perry Square
Erie, PA 16541

Rev. Carl F. Mengeling, Director
Institute of Religion,
St. Joseph Calumet College
4721 Indianapolis Boulevard
East Chicago, IN 46312

Rev. Arthur E. Rodgers, Director
Religious Studies Division
St. Charles Borromeo Seminary
Overbrook, PA 19151

Rev. John Miller, C.S.C.,
  Director
Institute of Catechetics and
  Spirituality
7887 Walmsley Avenue
New Orleans, LA 70125

A SPECIAL ORGANIZATION

Catholics United for the Faith, Inc.
222 North Avenue
New Rochelle, NY 10801

HOPE OF THE FAMILY
(OUR LADY OF AMERICA)

Holy Family Center
*write for booklet, insert and medal
(reasonable)*
New Riegel
Ohio 48853

APPENDIX II

CANISIUS CLUB

MODEL FOR A CATHOLIC BOOK REVIEW CLUB

Canisius Club is the name of a Catholic book review club, formed about forty years ago. The original chapter is still functioning. Canisius Club is named for St. Peter Canisius, Patron of Libraries. A secondary function of the club could be to establish a library with the books purchased for review. One could start loaning books with as few as a dozen titles.

One can start a chapter with four members, the ideal being twelve. With twelve members, a program can be set up for each month of the year. Each member would then be host or hostess once during the year, and would review one book a year, though arranged so hosting and reviewing would not be at the same meeting.

Dues would be used to purchase books for review, if not borrowed from a local Catholic or public library, or already in the possession of the reviewer.

The meeting would be opened with prayer, and chapters of the Canisius Club have used the following:

Hail Mary, etc.
Holy Mary, etc. Amen.
V. Holy Spirit
R. Enlighten us.

V. Seat of Wisdom
R. Pray for us.
V. St. Peter Canisius
R. Pray for us.

We might interpose here that "Canisius Club" is neither a copyright or registered name, so any group can use it. The chapter of the club ought to have its individual name also, such as Holy Spirit Chapter, St. Jerome Chapter, St. Francis of Assisi Chapter, and invoke the saint of the name taken, as well as, that of St. Peter Canisius in the prayers offered at the beginning of the meeting.

Included in our mimeographed chapter year book, besides, officers and program and hostesses for the year, together with the prayers, were included the following quotations:

WHY READ? "After the grace of God flaming to us through the channels of prayer and the Sacraments, I know no greater solace to the soul than the soothing words of a good book."

—Azarius

HOW TO READ: "If reading for self-improvement verify facts, consult authorities, make comparisons, get at the truth."

—Azarius

WHAT TO READ.

a) "In general: 'Do NOT read good books—Life is too short for that; read only the best.' "

—Dimnet

b) "In particular: 'Reading the newspaper is simply cramming of undigested facts in an attempt to become familiar in a quarter of an hour with issues it would take a life-time to master'."

—Azarius

We might add for the good of the nation.—

"Daniel Webster was 150 years ahead of his time when he said, 'If religious books are not widely circulated among the masses in this country, I do not know what is going to become of us as a nation. If truth be not diffused, error will be; if God and His word are not known and received, the devil and his works will gain the ascendency; if the evangelical volume does not reach every hamlet, the pages of a corrupt and licentious literature will; if the power of the Gospel is not felt throughout the length and breadth of the land, anarchy and misrule, degradation and misery, corruption and darkness, will reign without mitigation or end.' "

We have not heeded Daniel Webster, and so have gone down the path of degradation. But, there is hope. Let us all work toward a New Christendom.

BIBLIOGRAPHY

Attwater, Donald, Ed., *A Catholic Dictionary*. New York: Macmillan, c. 1931.

Bradley, Robert I., S.J. "Athanasias and the Arians." *Triumph*. Warrenton, Virginia: Society for the Christian Commonwealth, Inc. February 1974, p. 22f, and, March 1974, p. 24f.

Broderick, James, S.J., *Saint Peter Canisius*. New York: Sheed and Ward, 1938.

Daughters of St. Paul, *Where the Gospel Meets the World*. Boston: St. Paul Editions, 1977.

Foy, Felician A., O.F.M., ed. *1979 Catholic Almanac*. Huntington, Indiana: Our Sunday Visitor, Inc. 1978.

Geddes, Normal Bel, *Horizons*. Boston: Little, Brown and Co., 1932.

Grieco, Gianfranco, "A study by Cardinal Ballestrero—The Christian Family Vocation." *L'Osservatore Romano*, English Edition, 22 June 1981. p. 12.

Keane, J. R., O.S.M. *Marian Vignettes*. Washington, D.C., National Council of Catholic Men, 1939.

Lawler, Ronald, O.F.M., Cap., Donald W. Wuerl, Thomas Comeford Lawler, et al, editors, *The Teaching of Christ*. Huntington, Indiana: Our Sunday Visitor, Inc. 1976.

Leonard, Paul, S.J. "The Sacred Heart, the Rosary and the Domestic Church." *The Wanderer*. June 4, 1981.

Molnar, Thomas, *Utopia, the Perennial Heresy*. London: Tom Stacey, Ltd., c. 1971.

Nevins, Albert J., M M., compiler and editor, *The Maryknoll Catholic Dictionary*. New York: Grosset & Dunlap, 1965.

O'Brien, John A., "A Child's Small Prayerbook Led Family to Conversion." *The Voice*. Miami, Florida, April 13, 1962.

O'Hayer, Eileen, compiler, *The Catholic Travelers' Guide*. Chicago: Extension Magazine, 1954.

Oliveri, Marco, *The Representatives*. Gerrardo Cross: Van Duren Publishers, 1980.

Our Lady of America. New Riegel, Ohio: Cloistered Sisters of the Precious Blood, 1960, 1971.

Regamey Pie-Raymond, O.P., *What is an Angel?* Twentieth Century Encyclopedia of Catholicism. Vol. 47. New York Hawthorne Book Publishing Co., 1960.

Sill, Edward Rowland, "Opportunity." *Poems*. Cambridge: Riverside Press, 1900.

Stebbins, H. Lyman, "The Priesthood of the Laity in the 'Domestic Church.' " *Lay Witness*. New Rochelle, N.Y.: Catholics United for the Faith. July–August 1980.

Walsh, James J., *The Thirteenth Greatest of Centuries*. New York: Catholic Summer School Press, 1913.